ACT ASSESSMENT® ENGLISH

flash

ELAINE BENDER

PETERSON'S
THOMSON LEARNING™

Australia • Canada • Mexico • Singapore • Spain • United Kingdom • United States

About Peterson's

Founded in 1966, Peterson's, a division of Thomson Learning, is the nation's largest and most respected provider of lifelong learning online resources, software, reference guides, and books. The Education Supersite℠ at petersons.com—the Web's most heavily traveled education resource—has searchable databases and interactive tools for contacting U.S.-accredited institutions and programs. CollegeQuest® (CollegeQuest.com) offers a complete solution for every step of the college decision-making process. GradAdvantage™ (GradAdvantage.org), developed with Educational Testing Service, is the only electronic admissions service capable of sending official graduate test score reports with a candidate's online application. Peterson's serves more than 55 million education consumers annually.

Thomson Learning is among the world's leading providers of lifelong learning, serving the needs of individuals, learning institutions, and corporations with products and services for both traditional classrooms and for online learning. For more information about the products and services offered by Thomson Learning, please visit www.thomsonlearning.com. Headquartered in Stamford, Connecticut, with offices worldwide, Thomson Learning is part of The Thomson Corporation (www.thomson.com), a leading e-information and solutions company in the business, professional, and education marketplaces. The Corporation's common shares are listed on the Toronto and London stock exchanges.

An American BookWorks Corporation Project

For more information, contact Peterson's, 2000 Lenox Drive, Lawrenceville, NJ 08648; 800-338-3282; or find us on the World Wide Web at: www.petersons.com/about

Library of Congress Cataloging-in-Publication Data

Bender, Elaine.
[ACT English flash]
Peterson's ACT English flash / Elaine Bender.
p. cm.
Includes index.
ISBN 0-7689-0627-X
1. English language—Grammar—Examinations—Study guides. 2. Universities and colleges—United States—Entrance examinations—Study guides. 3. Language arts—Examinations—Study guides. 4. ACT Assessment—Study guides. I. Title.
PE1114.B434 1997
428′.0076—dc21 97-11301
CIP

Printed in Canada

10 9 8 7 6 5 4 3 2 1 03 02 01

CONTENTS

ABOUT ACT ENGLISH FLASH

You're getting ready to take the ACT exam and you need some last-minute practice. It's a well-known fact that the more you take replicas of the actual examination, the better you will do on the exam itself. Thus, here's a way to review the English portion of the ACT in a flash.

The questions in *ACT English Flash* are the same type of ACT questions that you'll encounter on the test. We have varied the difficulty of the questions, so that you will develop a "feel" for the test.

Using ACT English Flash

1. The *ACT English Flash* consists of two complete ACT English tests. A test consists of five passages with fifteen questions each, for a total of seventy-five questions. Within the passages there are words, phrases, and sentences that are underlined and numbered. The question numbers correspond to the numbers in the passage. You are given four choices about the underlined portion, one of which is usually "NO CHANGE." That means that you have not found anything wrong with that underlined portion, and it is correct as is.

   The other choices provide you with alternatives, if there is an error. Your job is to identify the error and select the appropriate selection. The explanations of the correct choices are provided, so that you can fully understand why the underlined portion was correct or needed to be corrected.

2. Complete all of the questions on each test. Just because you think a question is easy, don't skip it. You never know what might be lurking behind a seemingly innocent phrase. If you think it's easy, answer it anyway and check the answer. You can hope that you answered it correctly.

3. Remember that these are multiple-choice questions. What this means is that there is only one correct answer. Often there is one other answer that also seems correct, but of course, is not. In addition, the other choices may be very wrong, or slightly wrong.

4. It sometimes helps to repeat the sentence out loud (quietly, of course) and listen for the error, if there is one. Then substitute the different choices and say them out load also. You might be able to hear the correct choice.

The ACT English Test—And What To Expect!

By the time you are ready to take the ACT, you will have already learned the material that will be covered on the exam. The topics on this test are standard English grammar principles and the basics of standard written English. You will not be tested on things like spelling or vocabulary, as you would be on the SATs.

Content	Number of items	Percentage of English test
Usage/Mechanics	**40**	
Punctuation	10	13%
Grammar and Usage	12	16%
Sentence Structure	18	24%
Rhetorical Skills	**35**	
Strategy	12	16%
Organization	11	15%
Style	12	16%

You can see that the types of questions asked are balanced throughout the test, with slightly more questions about sentence structure. Essentially, you should be familiar with basic grammar principles, as well as rhetorical skills, which require some logic in your approach to the questions.

There is no magic when it comes to studying. What we have provided is a fast and easy way to test yourself, help you to focus on those areas that need additional study, and provide you with clear explanations of the types of questions you will encounter on the English portion of the ACT test. The best magic is practice.

Good luck!

TEST 1

DIRECTIONS: In the five passages that follow, certain words and phrases are underlined and numbered. Following the passage, you will find alternatives for each underlined part. You are to choose the one that best expresses the idea, makes the statement appropriate for standard written English, or is worded most consistently with the style and tone of the passage as a whole. If you think the original version is best, choose "NO CHANGE."

Passage 1

[1]

Some people shudder with fear when they think about spiders. Their eight legs and odd method of locomotion make them alien to those who walk on two legs. They trap their prey and spray it with digestive enzymes that break down the prey's body; then they suck up the nutritious liquid, a method of nutrition that may seem repulsive to humans. Additionally all spiders have fangs and are poisonous. Only six North American spiders, however, have a bite that can harm humans: they are the black, brown, red-legged and varied widow spiders, the sack spider, <u>and the brown recluse. The brown recluse is also known as the violin spider because of the shape of the markings on its back.</u> (1) <u>However, tarantulas make good pets.</u> (2)

[2]

A woman in California that doctors suspect was bitten by a
3
brown recluse spider suffered terrifying injuries. Her left leg was covered by a rash and was swollen, and she had symptoms similar to the flu. Admitted to a hospital, her condition deteriorated. She devel-
4
oped toxic shock syndrome. Doctors theorize that her infection was so severe that her body fought it at the expense of circulation of blood to her limbs eventually her arms and legs had to be amputated.
5

[3]

Although author Sue Hubbell, in her book *A Country Year*, writes
6
of being bitten by a brown recluse spider and surviving. In fact, her reaction only to the bite was a small pimple-shaped mark
7
as one might have after being bitten by a mosquito. A recluse spider's
8
bite can cause severe symptoms however, most people don't have a
9
serious reaction to the bite. Hubbell thinks people are making a
10
mountain out of a molehill.
10

[4]

In spite of the bad reputation, spiders are useful to humans. Because they eat and thus help to control insect pests.
11
[1] During the Second World War, spiders' silk was used in crosshairs
12
for gun sights, telescopes, and microscopes. [2] In ancient times,

compressed spider webs were put on wounds to stop the bleeding, and scientists today know the webs contain substances that discourage infections. [3] Like all living creatures, spiders have their most unique (13) niche in relation to all other beings in the biosphere. [4] They have provided other help to humans.

1. **(A)** NO CHANGE
   (B) and the brown recluse, the brown recluse is also known as the violin spider because of the shape of the markings on its back.
   (C) and the brown recluse, also known as the violin spider because of the shape of the markings on its back.
   (D) and the brown recluse, which is the spider that is also known as the violin spider because of the shape of the markings on its back.

2. The writer is thinking of eliminating this sentence. The best reason to do so is:
   (A) It does not explain why tarantulas are good pets.
   (B) The sentence is the shortest sentence in the paragraph.
   (C) "However" is not a logical transition word in context.
   (D) The paragraph is about why people fear spiders.

---

1. Ⓐ Ⓑ Ⓒ Ⓓ

2. Ⓐ Ⓑ Ⓒ Ⓓ

Answer #1: (C)

The correct answer is C. Answer B creates a comma splice, which is a serious error. A comma splice occurs when you try to connect two independent clauses with only a comma. You need to add a coordinate conjunction (such as "and" or "but"), to use a semicolon instead of a comma, or to begin a new sentence. Answers A and D repeat words and are wordy. Conciseness should be your aim. **(Style)**

Answer #2: (D)

The correct answer is D. Answer A will only compound the confusion if the sentence remains in the paragraph. Answers B and C do not relate the sentence to the paragraph. While Answer C is true, it is not the most important reason for omitting the sentence. **(Organization)**

3. **(A)** NO CHANGE
   (B) which
   (C) who
   (D) whom

4. **(A)** NO CHANGE
   (B) Admitted to a hospital, she began to feel worse.
   (C) Admitted to a hospital, her condition worsened.
   (D) Admitted to a hospital, she began to feel worser.

---

3. Ⓐ Ⓑ Ⓒ Ⓓ

4. Ⓐ Ⓑ Ⓒ Ⓓ

Answer #3: Ⓒ

The correct answer is C. "That" is not used with nonrestrictive (also known as nonessential) clauses, which provide information that is not absolutely necessary to complete the meaning of the sentence. "Which" is not used to refer to persons. Since the pronoun is the subject of "was bitten," use "who" (the nominative case) rather than "whom" (the objective case). **(Grammar and usage)**

Answer #4: Ⓑ

The correct answer is B. Answers A and C contain a dangling participle (Was her condition admitted to the hospital?). A dangling participle is a construction in which a participle (a verb form typically ending in -ed or -ing, used as an adjective) has no logical word to modify. Consider these examples: Playing the piano loudly, the candlesticks rattled and fell off. Were the candlesticks playing? Here is another example, which may be considered a misplaced modifier. On my way to school today, I saw several deer driving on Highway 100. Were the deer driving? Dangling participles can be amusing, and they are usually easy to remedy. Answer D contains an incorrect comparative form of "bad" ("worser"); the correct form is "worse." **(Sentence structure)**

5. **(A)** NO CHANGE
(B) limbs, eventually her arms and legs had to be amputated.
(C) limbs and eventually her arms and legs had to be amputated.
(D) limbs; eventually her arms and legs had to be amputated.

6. **(A)** NO CHANGE
(B) And author Sue Hubbell,
(C) Then, author Sue Hubbell
(D) However, author Sue Hubbell

5. (A) (B) (C) (D)

6. (A) (B) (C) (D)

Answer #5: Ⓓ

The correct answer is D. It includes a semicolon to attach an independent clause (''eventually her arms and legs had to be amputated'') to the main clause. Answer B includes a comma splice because it attempts to use only a comma to attach the independent clause to the main clause. Answer C creates a ''stringy sentence,'' which is often the result of merely inserting coordinate conjunctions to attach independent clauses to the main clause. This error is particularly obvious when coordinate conjunctions already appear in the sentence. **(Sentence structure)**

Answer #6: Ⓓ

The correct answer is D. Answer A is a sentence fragment because it does not express a complete thought. In Answers B and C, ''And'' and ''Then'' are not logical transitions to show the contrast between paragraphs [2] and [3]. Also try to avoid beginning a sentence with a coordinate conjunction such as ''and'' or ''but.'' **(Strategy)**

7. **(A)** NO CHANGE
(B) her reaction to only the bite
(C) only her reaction to the bite
(D) her only reaction to the bite

8. **(A)** NO CHANGE
(B) like the kind of pimple one might have
(C) like one might have
(D) as the kind of pimple one might have

7. (A) (B) (C) (D)

8. (A) (B) (C) (D)

Answer #7: (D)

The correct answer is D. Be careful about the use of "only," for writers can easily misplace it. In Answer A "only" modifies "her reaction"; "her reaction" only suggests there were other possible responses such as what she may have said. In Answer B "her reaction" was only to the bite rather than to other factors such as seeing the spider. In Answer C only "her reaction" suggests that there were others who could also have responded to the bite. Only is a versatile word; it can modify virtually any part of a sentence. **(Sentence structure)**

Answer #8: (C)

The correct answer is C. Answer A uses "as," a subordinating conjunction, instead of the preposition "like" to connect the noun clause "one might have" to the main clause. Answer B is wordy because it repeats "the kind of pimple." Answer D includes the subordinate conjunction "as" and is wordy like Answer B. **(Grammar and usage)**

9. **(A)** NO CHANGE
(B) symptoms; however, most
(C) symptoms, however, most
(D) symptoms. Most

10. **(A)** NO CHANGE
(B) building castles in the air.
(C) striking while the iron is hot.
(D) exaggerating the dangers they face.

9. (A) (B) (C) (D)

10. (A) (B) (C) (D)

Answer #9: (B)

The correct answer is B. Answer A is a fused or run-on sentence, which is the result of connecting independent clauses without any punctuation or conjunction. Answer C contains a comma splice; in this sentence "however" is a conjunctive adverb that must be preceded by a semicolon and followed by a comma because it is used to join independent clauses. Answer D corrects the fused sentence but reduces the paragraph's coherence by eliminating an important transition word "however." **(Sentence structure)**

Answer #10: (D)

The correct answer is D. All of the other choices are cliches, which are overused or worn-out expressions. Choose a fresh, original way to express your ideas whenever possible. You should avoid cliches. Also, since three of the choices here are cliches, you should see the similarities and avoid the trap of making an incorrect choice. **(Style)**

11. **(A)** NO CHANGE
(B) humans; because they eat and thus help to control insect pests.
(C) humans: because they eat and thus help to control insect pests.
(D) humans because they eat and thus help to control insect pests.

12. **(A)** NO CHANGE
(B) During the Second World War, spiders
(C) During the second world war, spiders'
(D) During the Second World War, spider's

11. (A) (B) (C) (D)

12. (A) (B) (C) (D)

Answer #11: Ⓓ

The correct answer is D. Answer A is a sentence fragment, which means that it is not a complete sentence. "Because they eat and thus help to control insect pests" is a dependent adverb clause; it cannot stand alone as a complete sentence. To correct this kind of error, you can simply join the clause to the main clause, which in this instance precedes the fragment. No special punctuation is needed in many cases. Answer B is incorrect because the semicolon is misused; a subordinate conjunction ("because") is in place. Use either a semicolon or a subordinate conjunction. Answer C is incorrect because a colon is misused. This mark of punctuation typically is used to precede a list, not to connect a dependent clause to a main clause. **(Sentence structure)**

Answer #12: Ⓐ

The correct answer is A. Answer B needs an apostrophe to follow "spiders" to form the plural possessive form. Answer C contains capitalization errors; "second world war" should be capitalized because it names a specific war, such as the Civil War. Answer D offers the singular possessive ("spider's") rather than the plural form. **(Grammar and usage)**

13. **(A)** NO CHANGE
(B) unique
(C) uniquest
(D) uniquer

14. The correct order for the sentences in paragraph 4 is:

(A) NO CHANGE
(B) 3, 1, 2, 4
(C) 1, 2, 4, 3
(D) 4, 1, 2, 3

13. (A) (B) (C) (D)

14. (A) (B) (C) (D)

Answer #13: Ⓑ

The correct answer is B. "Unique" means only one exists; it has no comparative ("more") or superlative ("most") form. Other similar words are "true" and "perfect." Another aspect you need to watch for is the choice between using -er and -est and using more and most. Usually one- and two-syllable adjectives form the comparative and superlative in this manner. For instance, consider these examples: big, bigger, biggest—happy, happier, happiest. To form the comparative and superlative forms for words of three syllables or more, use more and most as in these examples: beautiful, more beautiful, most beautiful—wonderful, more wonderful, most wonderful. **(Grammar and usage)**

Answer #14: Ⓓ

The correct answer is D. Sentence 4 connects the first sentence of the paragraph with Sentences 1 and 2, and Sentence 3 enlarges the context from spiders' help to humans to spiders' roles in the environment. **(Organization)**

15. Item 15 poses a question about the passage as a whole. The passage's purpose is best described as:

(A) Contrasting the images of spiders with facts about spiders
(B) Explaining the threat of the recluse spider to humans
(C) Showing how spiders got their bad reputations
(D) Describing the behavior of spiders

---

15. 

Answer #15: Ⓓ

The correct answer is D. Answer A is correct in that some contrasts are presented; however, these contrasts are not the main idea of the passage. Answer B limits the main idea too much as it focuses only on the brown recluse spider. Answer C is similarly too narrow with its focus on "bad reputations." **(Strategy)**

Passage 2

[1]

Nevertheless, [16] Alice asks him if he can explain the poem "Jabberwocky" to her. She had read the poem in the White King's memorandum book. Humpty Dumpty explains that some of the hard words in the poem is [17] "portmanteau" words. A portmanteau is a suitcase or traveling bag to carry clothing in while traveling. So a word, which combines the meaning of two words in one, [18] is a portmanteau word.

[2]

Humpty Dumpty's first example from the poem is "slithy." It is a combination of the words "lithe," which means active, and "slimy." Another adjective he explains is "mimsy." Which combines [19] flimsy and miserable. Humpty Dumpty does not define all of the portmanteau words in the poem. Readers can decide for themselves what two words are packed in Carrolls [20] portmanteaus.

[3]

Is "frumious" a combination of furious and fuming? Or does it combine frugal and mysterious? Was Ebenezer Scrooge frumious! [21] Does to "galumph" mean to gallop and stumbling at the same time? [22] Does it describe a clumsy horse? Clearly a "frabjous" day, which combines fabulous and joyous, ain't [23] a sad one.

[4]

None of these words have (24) survived outside of "Jabberwocky." But one word in the poem has become a part of normal English vocabulary. To "chortle," is to chuckle or utter with glee. The words derivation according to dictionaries (25) is the combination of "chuckle" and "snort," and Lewis Carroll is given credit for having coined the word.

[5]

Humpty Dumpty, in Lewis Carroll's "Through The Looking Glass," becomes involved in a dialogue about the meaning of words with Alice. (26) He says unbirthdays are better than birthdays, because you have only one of the latter and 364 of the former. He says that is "glory" and he defines glory as (27) "there's a nice knockdown argument for you!" When Alice complains that isn't what glory means, he replies "When I use a word, it means just what I choose it to mean—neither more nor less." Thus he seems like an odd creature to ask about meanings.

16. **(A)** NO CHANGE
(B) Thus.
(C) Moreover,
(D) Anyway,

17. **(A)** NO CHANGE
(B) is: "portmanteau:"
(C) are "portmanteau"
(D) are: "portmanteau"

16. (A) (B) (C) (D)

17. (A) (B) (C) (D)

Answer #16: Ⓐ

The correct answer is A. The choice in this question depends on the introductory word and its function. "Nevertheless" shows a contrast. Answers B and C do not show the relationship between this paragraph and the one preceding it when the paragraphs are arranged in the correct order. "Thus" sets up a causal sequence while "moreover" suggests additional information. Answer D is too colloquial in tone to fit the passage. Colloquial language is what we use speaking informally as in conversations with friends and families. The style of this passage is more formal. **(Style)**

Answer #17: Ⓒ

The correct answer is C. The subject of the verb in this sentence is "some." This indefinite pronoun can be either singular or plural, depending on the prepositional phrase that follows it. Here the phrase "of the hard words" makes "some" plural because "words" can be counted. If the prepositional phrase following "some" had been "of the water," then the pronoun "some" would be singular, since "water" cannot be counted. It can be measured instead to show how much: a cup of water or a gallon of water, for instance. Consider these other examples: some of the flour or coffee (singular); some of the cookies or pencils (plural). Answer A, therefore, is wrong because of the subject-verb agreement error. Answers B and D incorrectly use a colon after a linking verb. No punctuation should separate a linking verb and its complement (predicate nominative or predicate adjective). **(Grammar and usage)**

18. **(A)** NO CHANGE
(B) word, which combines the meaning of two words in one
(C) word which combines the meaning of two words in one,
(D) word which combines the meaning of two words in one

19. **(A)** NO CHANGE
(B) "mimsy" which
(C) "mimsy," which
(D) "mimsy", which

18. (A) (B) (C) (D)

19. (A) (B) (C) (D)

Answer #18: (D)

The correct answer is D. The clause, "which combines the meaning of two words in one," is a restrictive clause, essential to the meaning of the sentence. Without this clause the sentence would be "So a word is a portmanteau word." "Word" is not sufficiently explained without the essential or restrictive clause. It should not be set off by commas as Answers A, B, and C do. **(Punctuation)**

Answer #19: (C)

The correct answer is C. Answer A is a sentence fragment; "Which combines flimsy and miserable" does not express a complete thought. Answer B needs a comma to separate the adjective clause from the main clause. Answer D has a punctuation error: the comma should always be placed within the quotation marks. **(Sentence structure)**

20. **(A)** NO CHANGE
(B) in, Carrolls
(C) in Carroll's
(D) in, Carroll's

21. **(A)** NO CHANGE
(B) Scrooge frumious.
(C) Scrooge frumious:
(D) Scrooge frumious?

20. (A) (B) (C) (D)

21. (A) (B) (C) (D)

Answer #20: (C)

The correct answer is C. The apostrophe is required to show possession for "Carrolls." The singular form of the word is "Carroll"; an apostrophe plus *s* correctly forms the possessive form. Answer A lacks an apostrophe for "Carrolls." Answer B incorrectly inserts a comma between the preposition "in" and its object ("Carrolls," which should have an apostrophe to show possession). Answer D presents the correct possessive form, but it also incorrectly includes a comma between the preposition and its object. **(Punctuation)**

Answer #21: (D)

The correct answer is D. Because the sentence is a question, a question mark must follow it. The other answers do not treat the sentence as a question. Answer A treats the sentence as an exclamation. Answer B ends in a period, the mark of punctuation that ends a declarative sentence. Answer C incorrectly includes a colon, which ordinarily precedes a list instead of ending a sentence or connecting independent clauses. **(Punctuation)**

22. **(A)** NO CHANGE
(B) to gallop and to stumble at the same time
(C) galloping and stumbling at the same time
(D) galloping and to stumble at the same time

23. **(A)** NO CHANGE
(B) aren't
(C) am not
(D) isn't

22. (A) (B) (C) (D)

23. (A) (B) (C) (D)

Answer #22: Ⓑ

The correct answer is B. To maintain the parallel sentence construction of the first part of the sentence, "Does to 'galumph . . . ,' " you need the infinitive forms "to gallop and to stumble." Only Answer B includes two infinitives. The other answers include either gerunds or a combination of infinitive and gerund. Infinitives and gerunds are verb forms that function as other parts of speech. Infinitives (formed by "to" plus a verb) can be used as adjectives, adverbs, or nouns. Gerunds (verb forms ending in -ing) can be used as nouns. In the sentence for Question 22, it would also be correct to say, "Does to 'galumph' mean galloping and stumbling at the same time" because you would be using two gerunds. Parallelism in writing means being consistent in the kinds of structure you use, especially in compound constructions. **(Grammar and usage)**

Answer #23: Ⓓ

The correct answer is D. Answer A, while often used in conversation, is inappropriate in written context unless used humorously or in dialogue. Answer B creates an agreement error; the subject of the sentence ("day") is singular; "aren't" is plural. Answer C shifts the person of the verb from third (he, she, it) to first person (I). **(Style)**

24. **(A)** NO CHANGE
(B) is
(C) are
(D) has

25. **(A)** NO CHANGE
(B) word's derivation according to dictionaries
(C) words derivation, according to dictionaries
(D) word's derivation, according to dictionaries,

24. (A) (B) (C) (D)

25. (A) (B) (C) (D)

Answer #24: (D)

The correct answer is D. The subject of the sentence is "none," which requires a singular verb. Answer B changes from active to passive voice; the sense of the sentence is that no word has survived. "Is survived" shifts to passive voice, a verb form in which the subject receives the action of the verb. Answers A and C incorrectly offer plural verbs in subject-verb agreement. **(Grammar and usage)**

Answer #25: (D)

The correct answer is D. The apostrophe is needed to show possession, and since the phrase "according to dictionaries" is not essential to the meaning of the sentence, it should be set off by commas. Answer A offers neither of the necessary punctuation marks. Answer B fails to set off the prepositional phrase by commas. Answer C omits the apostrophe needed to show possession. **(Punctuation)**

26. **(A)** NO CHANGE
(B) dialogue with Alice about the meaning of words.
(C) dialogue of words with Alice.
(D) dialogue about the meaning of words to Alice.

27. **(A)** NO CHANGE
(B) "glory", and he defines glory as
(C) "glory," and he defines glory as
(D) "glory: and he defines glory as

26. (A) (B) (C) (D)

27. (A) (B) (C) (D)

Answer #26: Ⓑ

The correct answer is B. In Answer A, "with Alice" is misplaced; it modifies "words." Try to be sure that modifiers are located as closely as possible to the words they modify. Answer C changes the meaning of the sentence: a "dialogue of words" does not address the key issue of meaning. In Answer D "to Alice," also changes the meaning of the original sentence. In this version the focus is on what Alice thinks the words mean. **(Sentence structure)**

Answer #27: Ⓒ

The correct answer is C. Answer A is a fused or run-on sentence because there is no comma preceding "and" to separate the independent clauses. Answer B also includes a punctuation error; the comma is misplaced after the quotation marks. Answer D incorrectly includes a colon to join the independent clauses. **(Sentence structure)**

28. The writer is thinking of adding the following sentences to the passage: "And what kind of sound is "burbling?" Is it babbling and murmuring, or is it blubbering and warbling?" This sentence should be added in which paragraph?

(A) Paragraph 1
(B) Paragraph 2
(C) Paragraph 3
(D) Paragraph 4

29. The proper sequence for the paragraphs in this passage is:

(A) NO CHANGE
(B) 5, 1, 3, 2, 4
(C) 2, 3, 5, 1, 4
(D) 5, 1, 2, 3, 4

---

28. Ⓐ Ⓑ Ⓒ Ⓓ

29. Ⓐ Ⓑ Ⓒ Ⓓ

Answer #28: (D)

The correct answer is D, because it is the paragraph that gives examples of possible meanings for portmanteau words. **(Organization)**

Answer #29: (D)

The correct answer is D. Paragraph 5 offers a sound introduction that leads to the subject of the words in the poem. The other paragraphs follow in logical order. **(Organization)**

30. The main purpose of this passage is to:

(A) describe the character of Humpty Dumpty.
(B) explain what portmanteau words are.
(C) advance the plot of "Alice Through the Looking Glass."
(D) analyze the poem "Jabberwocky."

---

30. 

Answer #30: Ⓑ

The correct answer is B. No other answer describes all of the content of the passage. Answer A is limited to Humpty Dumpty, who is not the focus of the passage; Answer C is incorrect because the passage does not serve to relate the plot of the poem; Answer D is incorrect because there is no real analysis of "Jabberwocky" here. **(Strategy)**

Passage 3

[1]

No one would deny that adolescence is a difficult stage. You know that adolescence has arrived when you wake up one morning and your pajamas are too short. You walk to the bathroom and look at yourself in the <u>mirror, and notice</u> (31) a red spot on one of your <u>cheeks you panic</u> (32) and reach for your Oxy 85 to take care of it. <u>Having cared for your face, your body is next</u> (33). You take off your pajamas to shower, and to your amazement, some sort of hair has grown overnight on your body. <u>One runs to one's desk</u> (34) to find a book to explain what has happened; then you realize what it is. The hair is a sign you are maturing physically. You hurry to school to share this great discovery with your friends. Some of them are curious, but some of them are not impressed <u>at all, because they have</u> (35) already experienced <u>the same thing</u> (36).

[2]

<u>Adolescence, besides causing physical changes</u> (37), creates social dilemmas. You become <u>more awarer</u> (38) of the opposite sex. You wonder <u>how to go about to ask for</u> (39) a date with the person you like. Your friends already have dates for the school dance on <u>Saturday but you,</u> (40) are still trying to decide whether to make that phone call. If you get a negative response, you can simply tell your friends that you would

rather stay home to watch the Charlie Brown special on television. You have always enjoyed the Peanuts cartoons. (41) You could even tell them you'll be reading the article about the hot new trends in your favorite area, whether they are sci-fi films, rap music, or skateboards. (42)

[3]

[1] When you finish high school and start college, making your own decisions and taking responsibilities for your actions, you smile and realize there is life after adolescence. [2] But another emotion is mixed with your pride. [3] If I had the resources, I would give all junior and senior high school students stickers that read "I may be getting older, but I refuse to grow up." [4] In spite of all its problems and confusions, adolescence permits you to retain some of the spontaneity of childhood. (43)

31. **(A)** NO CHANGE
(B) mirror and notice
(C) mirror and you notice
(D) mirror. And notice

32. **(A)** NO CHANGE
(B) cheeks, you panic
(C) cheeks. Panicking
(D) cheeks. You panic

31. (A) (B) (C) (D)

32. (A) (B) (C) (D)

Answer #31: Ⓑ

The correct answer is B. The subject of "notice" is the first word in the sentence ("You"). "Notice" is part of a compound predicate, "walk and look and notice." Thus, no comma is needed because the parts of the predicate are connected by "and." Answer C could be correct if it included a comma before "and"; as written, however, it needlessly repeats the subject. Answer D creates a sentence fragment because it begins with a coordinate conjunction. **(Punctuation)**

Answer #32: Ⓓ

The correct answer is D. Answer A creates a run-on or fused sentence. Answer B is a comma splice because a comma is used to connect independent clauses. Answer C possibly creates a dangling participle because the subject of the second sentence is unknown. A dangling participle is a construction in which a participle (a verb form typically ending in -ed or -ing, used as an adjective) has no logical word to modify. **(Sentence structure)**

33. **(A)** NO CHANGE
(B) Your body is next, having cared for your face.
(C) Having cared for your face, you think of your body.
(D) Having cared for you face and body.

34. **(A)** NO CHANGE
(B) One runs to your desk
(C) One runs to ones desk
(D) You run to your desk

33. (A) (B) (C) (D)

34. (A) (B) (C) (D)

Answer #33: Ⓒ

The correct answer is C. In Answers A and B, there is no word for "having cared for your body" to modify logically; both answers create dangling participles. Answer D is a sentence fragment because it does not express a complete thought. **(Sentence structure)**

Answer #34: Ⓓ

The correct answer is D. To avoid the shifts in person in Answers A and B, choose D because it maintains a second person point of view ("you"). Answers A and B use third ("one"). Answer C is also incorrect because it omits an apostrophe in the possessive form of "ones." Even if the apostrophe were there, the shift from "you" to "one" makes this choice an incorrect one. **(Style)**

35. **(A)** NO CHANGE
(B) at all. Because they have
(C) at all, because they are
(D) at all, because they be

36. **(A)** NO CHANGE
(B) this phenomenon.
(C) bodily changes.
(D) hairiness.

35. (A) (B) (C) (D)

36. (A) (B) (C) (D)

Answer #35: (A)

The correct answer is A. Answer B creates a sentence fragment; "Because they have already experienced the same thing" does not express a complete thought. Answers C and D use incorrect verb forms as auxiliary or "helping" verbs. **(Punctuation)**

Answer #36: (B)

The correct answer is B. Answer A is vague; avoid using "thing" in your writing whenever you can. Answer C is too vague, and Answer D is too specific. **(Style)**

37. **(A)** NO CHANGE
(B) Adolescence besides causing physical changes
(C) Adolescence, besides causing physical changes
(D) Adolescence besides causing physical changes, it

38. **(A)** NO CHANGE
(B) awarer
(C) more aware
(D) awarest

37. (A) (B) (C) (D)

38. (A) (B) (C) (D)

Answer #37: Ⓐ

The correct answer is A. Since the phrase is not essential to the meaning of the sentence, it should be set off by commas. Answers B, C, and D include comma errors by either misplacing or omitting the commas, which should precede and follow the prepositional phrase "besides causing physical changes." **(Punctuation)**

Answer #38: Ⓒ

The correct answer is C. While the comparative form of two-syllable words is typically formed by adding -er, if the accent is on the second syllable, the comparative is formed by using "more." For instance, the comparative form of "happy" is "happier," but the comparative form of "unfair" is "more unfair." **(Grammar and usage)**

39. **(A)** NO CHANGE
(B) how to go about the task of asking for
(C) how to go about asking for
(D) how to ask for

40. **(A)** NO CHANGE
(B) Saturday, but you,
(C) Saturday. But you
(D) Saturday, but you

39. Ⓐ Ⓑ Ⓒ Ⓓ

40. Ⓐ Ⓑ Ⓒ Ⓓ

Answer #39: (D)

The correct answer is D. The other choices are unnecessarily wordy. Try to express ideas as concisely and clearly as possible. **(Style)**

Answer #40: (D)

The correct answer is D. Answer A creates a fused or run-on sentence and incorrectly uses a comma to separate the subject and verb in the second clause. Answer B corrects the run-on but also includes the unnecessary comma after "you." Answer C weakens the connection between the two sentences by dividing them into two separate sentences. Also, you should try to avoid beginning sentences with coordinate conjunctions such as "but" or "and." Inserting a conjunctive adverb, such as "however" or "nevertheless," between the subject and verb of the sentence can provide more effective transition. **(Sentence structure)**

41. The writer should omit this sentence because:

(A) Adolescents are too old to watch cartoons on television.
(B) The sentence is the shortest one in the paragraph.
(C) The sentence is not relevant to the paragraph's main idea.
(D) The sentence should be placed earlier in the paragraph.

42. **(A)** NO CHANGE
(B) whether it is sci-fi films, rap music, or skateboards.
(C) whether your favorite area is sci-fi films, rap music, or skateboards.
(D) whether they are sci-fi films rap music or skateboards.

---

41. (A) (B) (C) (D)

42. (A) (B) (C) (D)

Answer #41: (C)

The correct answer is C. The information presented here is not relevant to the paragraph. Answer B is illogical; the length of a sentence does not show its merit. Answer D offers illogical advice; a different placement will not remedy the irrelevance of the sentence. **(Organization)**

Answer #42: (B)

The correct answer is B. Since "area" is singular, you need a singular pronoun in the dependent clause. Answer C is wordy because it needlessly repeats "your favorite area." Answer D omits necessary commas between items in a series. **(Grammar and mechanics)**

43. Should the writer omit sentence [4] from this paragraph?

(A) Yes, because it is too general.
(B) Yes, because it introduces a new idea to the essay.
(C) No, because it summarizes the content of the whole essay.
(D) No, because it provides a conclusion, which refers to earlier content.

44. The writer wants to add the sentence "Now you are an adult" to this paragraph. The best place to add it is after sentence:

(A) [1]
(B) [2]
(C) [3]
(D) [4]

43. (A) (B) (C) (D)

44. (A) (B) (C) (D)

Answer #43: (B)

The correct answer is B. The "spontaneity of childhood" is not discussed in the paragraph (or in the entire passage, for that matter). Answer A is not relevant. Answers C and D likewise are inappropriate. **(Strategy)**

Answer #44: (A)

The correct answer is A. It provides effective transition between sentences [1] and [3] by helping to develop ideas smoothly. **(Organization)**

45. Would this passage fulfill an assignment asking a student to write an essay defining adolescence?

(A) No, because it is too short to be an essay.
(B) Yes, because it talks about you and adolescence.
(C) No, because it is a different definition than would be found in a dictionary.
(D) Yes, because it defines the word from the author's point of view.

45. 

Answer #45: (D)

The correct answer is D. This essay does offer a definition of adolescence from the author's point of view. Answer A is irrelevant; quantity does not equal quality. Answer B is too general; "talking about adolescence" is not the same as defining it. Answer C does not pertain to the question; whether the denotation (dictionary definition) differs from your definition is not important. **(Strategy)**

Passage 4

[1]

Sixteen years after his death, in 1995, John Wayne was ranked first in a Harris poll that asked Americans "Who is your favorite male movie star?" People have speculated about the reasons for Wayne's enduring popularity. One theory is that Wayne's popularity ensures [46] because of the image his characters presented. This [47] was captured by the gold medal Congress struck after his death in 1979. It read "John Wayne, American."

[2]

Most of his films were westerns or war films. However, he was not always the same character. In *Stagecoach*, he is a naive; in *Red River,* he is a capitalist; and in *The Shootist,* he is a retired gunfighter dying of cancer. He can be an officer in the Pacific during the Second World War, as he was in *Sands of Iwo Jima* and *Flying Leathernecks*, or, as in *True Grit*, a fat old drunk marshal. For which role he won the best actor Academy Award in 1969 [48]. Even when he was not playing a soldier or a cowboy, as in *The Quiet Man*, he has the virtues associated with the American frontier: individualism [49], honesty, and a willingness to fight and die for what he believes in. Shortly after Wayne's [50] death, President Jimmy Carter describe Wayne as "a symbol of many of the most basic qualities that made America great. The ruggedness, the

tough independence, the sense of personal conviction and courage . . . reflected the best of <u>our national character''.</u> In a time when Ameri-
51
cans wonder whether the values that created our nation endure, the image of American manhood presented in his movies <u>are reassuring.</u>
52

[3]

His image was enhanced by his physical qualities and abilities as an actor. He was a big man, and his size and strength suggested his power and authority. Yet he moved with grace, and he knew how to use <u>his body, it wasn't only</u> that he looked comfortable riding a horse.
53
The sense he conveyed of being totally at ease with himself physically reinforced his <u>aura of invincibility and his voice</u> cannot be forgotten.
54
His speech has a stop-and-go rhythm <u>which speaks softly but carries a big stick.</u>
55

[4]

<u>Although some Americans have begun to ask if Wayne is the hero for all Americans.</u> They point out that his virtues are those typically
56
associated with masculinity and aggressiveness. His characters are not insensitive nor are they cruel to women. But in Wayne's America, women knew their place. His western films stereotyped Native-Americans, and in his war films, the enemy <u>were</u> portrayed as evil,
57
inhuman monsters from backward countries.

[5]

However, even with the recognition that Wayne may not embody the values appropriate to late-twentieth-century and early twenty-first century America, it is likely that his films will continue to be watched and enjoyed. 60

46. (A) NO CHANGE
(B) endures
(C) ensues
(D) insures

47. (A) NO CHANGE
(B) That
(C) His character
(D) That image

46. (A) (B) (C) (D)

47. (A) (B) (C) (D)

Answer #46: (B)

The correct answer is B. "Endures" here means "lasts" or "persists." The other choices are not logical options. "Ensues" means "follows"; "insures" means "guarantees." Read all of the choices carefully. **(Style)**

Answer #47: (D)

The correct answer is D. Answers A and B are vague because neither has a clear antecedent, which is the word the pronoun replaces or to which it refers. Watch out for words like "this," "that," and "which," and be sure that each pronoun has a clear antecedent. Correcting this kind of error usually involves including a noun. Answer C changes the meaning of the sentence. **(Style)**

48. (A) NO CHANGE
(B) marshal: for which role he won the best actor Academy Award in 1969.
(C) marshal, for which role he won the best actor Academy Award in 1969.
(D) marshal for which he won the best actor Academy Award in 1969.

49. (A) NO CHANGE
(B) frontier; individualism
(C) frontier, individualism,
(D) frontier. Individualism,

48. (A) (B) (C) (D)

49. (A) (B) (C) (D)

Answer #48: Ⓒ

The correct answer is C. Answer A contains a sentence fragment, and Answer B incorrectly uses a colon to connect the clauses. Answer D does not include the necessary comma. **(Sentence structure)**

Answer #49: Ⓐ

The correct answer is A. Answer B incorrectly uses a semicolon to introduce the formal list. Answer C offers a similar error by using a comma to introduce the list. Answer D incorrectly begins a new sentence by capitalizing "individualism," but this approach creates a sentence fragment. **(Punctuation)**

50. **(A)** NO CHANGE
(B) Waynes'
(C) Waynes
(D) Way'nes

51. **(A)** NO CHANGE
(B) our national character"
(C) our national character."
(D) our national character.

50. (A) (B) (C) (D)

51. (A) (B) (C) (D)

Answer #50: Ⓐ

The correct answer is A. This choice presents the correct spelling of the singular possessive form. Answer B is the plural possessive form. Answer C does not show possession. Answer D includes a punctuation error. **(Punctuation)**

Answer #51: Ⓒ

The correct answer is C. This choice correctly places the period inside the quotation marks. In Answer A the placement of the quotation marks and the period is reversed. Answer B lacks a period to end the sentence. Answer D omits the closing quotation marks. Be sure to look carefully at the way quotation marks are used with other marks of punctuation. **(Punctuation)**

52. **(A)** NO CHANGE
(B) have reassuring.
(C) were reassuring.
(D) is reassuring.

53. **(A)** NO CHANGE
(B) his body; it wasn't only
(C) his body it wasn't only
(D) his body and it wasn't only

52. (A) (B) (C) (D)

53. (A) (B) (C) (D)

Answer #52: (D)

The correct answer is D. The subject of the verb is "image," which is singular. The other choices offer errors with subject-verb agreement. **(Grammar and usage)**

Answer #53: (B)

The correct answer is B. Answer A creates a comma splice by connecting two independent clauses by a comma. Answers C and D create run-on or fused sentences because the necessary punctuation is missing. **(Sentence structure)**

54. **(A)** NO CHANGE
(B) aura of invincibility: his voice
(C) aura of invincibility his voice
(D) aura of invincibility, and his voice

55. **(A)** NO CHANGE
(B) strikes while the iron is hot.
(C) shows how good and strong of a man that he was.
(D) demonstrates his authority.

54. (A) (B) (C) (D)

55. (A) (B) (C) (D)

Answer #54: Ⓓ

The correct answer is D. Answer A creates a run-on or fused sentence because it omits necessary punctuation between the independent clauses. Answer B incorrectly uses a colon to connect the independent clauses. Answer C is also a run-on or fused sentence. **(Sentence structure)**

Answer #55: Ⓓ

The correct answer is D. Answers A and B are cliches or trite expressions. They lack originality. Answer C is verbose; useless words obscure meaning. **(Style)**

56. **(A)** NO CHANGE
(B) Thus, some Americans have begun to ask if Wayne is the hero for all Americans.
(C) However, some Americans have begun to ask if Wayne is the hero for all Americans.
(D) Although some Americans have begun to ask if Wayne is the hero for all Americans:

57. **(A)** NO CHANGE
(B) has
(C) is
(D) are

56. (A) (B) (C) (D)

57. (A) (B) (C) (D)

Answer #56: Ⓒ

The correct answer is C. Answer A is a sentence fragment; it cannot stand alone as a complete sentence. Answer B offers a correct sentence, but in this context "thus" is not used logically for transition. Answer D misuses a colon to connect the clauses. **(Sentence structure)**

Answer #57: Ⓐ

The correct answer is A. "Enemy" is a collective noun that can be considered singular or plural, depending on the context. Here, "evil, inhuman monsters" indicates that "enemy" is plural. Answers B and C are wrong choices, because they incorrectly offer the singular form of the verb. Answer D is incorrect because, although it includes the plural form of the verb, it shifts from past to present tense. **(Grammar and usage)**

58. The writer is thinking of adding the following sentence to the passage: "Part of Wayne's appeal is a nostalgia for a simpler America, which people believe existed in the past." The best place to add this sentence is:

(A) As the first sentence in paragraph 1
(B) As the last sentence of paragraph 1
(C) As the last sentence of paragraph 3
(D) As the first sentence of paragraph 4

59. The best title for this essay is:

(A) John Wayne—Movie Star
(B) John Wayne—American
(C) John Wayne—A Man For Today?
(D) John Wayne—The Western Hero

---

58. (A) (B) (C) (D)

59. (A) (B) (C) (D)

Answer #58: (D)

The correct answer is D. Placing the sentence there provides a transition from a description of Wayne's reputation in the past to a contemporary view of John Wayne. **(Organization)**

Answer #59: (B)

The correct answer is B. It most accurately states the main idea of the passage. Answer A incorrectly limits the main idea to his involvement in movies. Answer C overemphasizes his popularity today. Answer D also limits the main idea to Wayne's role in westerns. **(Strategy)**

60. This sentence should be added to paragraph 4 because:

(A) Ordinarily, a sentence standing alone is not a complete paragraph.
(B) Paragraph 4 lacks a concluding sentence.
(C) The sentence unifies the essay by returning to the idea of Wayne's popularity.
(D) All of the above.

---

60. 

Answer #60: Ⓓ

The correct answer is D. The sentence will provide a concluding sentence for Paragraph 4. It unifies the essay by returning to the idea of Wayne's popularity, and a sentence standing alone is typically not a complete paragraph. **(Organization)**

Passage 5

[1]

Because I am in the early stage of my career as a violinist. Most of my contracts (61) with symphony orchestras have been for periods of time ranging from the shortest of six months to the longest of two years. (62) Thus, I have had to move (63) from my home base in Los Angeles quite often. I have played with orchestras in Rochester, New York; Canton, Ohio, Seattle, Washington; Munich, Germany; and Durban, South Africa. (64) The business of moving has several phases. There is a period of denial, then (65) I find myself angry and hostile about the future. I feel I am slowly disintegrating, unable to eat or sleep. I scream at other drivers for things I could care less about. (66)

[2]

Longing for things to stay as they are, I look at every view of palm trees against a stunning mountain backdrop as a work of art. I drive to the old neighborhoods where I lived when I was a child. As often as I can, I go out to eat Mexican food. I cruise Sunset Boulevard and then drive to Pasadena to revisit my high school. I drop in on my first violin teacher, with whom I have always kept in touch. (68)

[3]

[1] I begin to accept my situation. [2] I make necessary phone calls. [3] Leave a change of address notice at the post office, and sign my mom onto my bank account. [4] I make arrangements for a friend to store my car until I decide what to do with it. [5] I gladly cancel my car insurance. [6] I pay the telephone company an exorbitant fee to refer calls to my parents phone number. [7] I have given my landlord thirty days' notice, make arrangements for my accountant to do my taxes when the time comes, and cancel my newspaper and magazine subscriptions. [8] I even suspend my cellular phone service and my pager. [9] I try to see my friends and family frequently before I leave. [10] Trying to ignore the sadness of good-byes, I promise to write to them often.

(Underlined portions: "phone calls. [3] Leave a change of address notice at the post office, and sign" — 70; "parents phone number." — 71; "have given" — 72; "Trying to ignore the sadness of good-byes, I promise to write to them often." — 75)

61. **(A)** NO CHANGE
(B) Because I am in the early stage of my career as a violinist; Most of my contracts
(C) Because I am in the early stage of my career as a violinist; most of my contracts
(D) Because I am in the early stage of my career as a violinist, most of my contracts

62. **(A)** NO CHANGE
(B) for time spans ranging from six months to two long years.
(C) for varying periods of time.
(D) for short terms of six months to two years.

61. Ⓐ Ⓑ Ⓒ Ⓓ

62. Ⓐ Ⓑ Ⓒ Ⓓ

Answer #61: Ⓓ

The correct answer is D. Answer A is a sentence fragment because "Because I am in the early stage of my career as a violinist" does not express a complete thought. Answer B misuses a semicolon to connect a dependent clause to an independent clause, and it incorrectly capitalizes "Most." Answer C also misuses a semicolon to connect a dependent clause to an independent clause. **(Sentence structure)**

Answer #62: Ⓓ

The correct answer is D. Answer A is wordy; Answer B only slightly reduces the wordiness. Answer C is vague. Answer D succinctly describes the time span. **(Style)**

63. **(A)** NO CHANGE
(B) I am moved
(C) I have had to moving
(D) I be moving

64. **(A)** NO CHANGE
(B) I have played with orchestras in Rochester, New York; Canton, Ohio; Seattle, Washington; Munich, Germany; and Durban, South Africa.
(C) I have played with orchestras in Rochester; New York; Canton; Ohio; Seattle; Washington; Munich; Germany; and Durban; South Africa.
(D) I have played with orchestras in Rochester, New York, Canton, Ohio, Seattle, Washington, Munich, Germany, and Durban, South Africa.

---

63. (A) (B) (C) (D)

64. (A) (B) (C) (D)

Answer #63: (A)

The correct answer is A. Answer B shifts from active voice to passive voice ("I am moved" by whom?). Answer C incorrectly uses the -ing form of "move" instead of the infinitive ("to move"). Answer D is an incorrect verb form. **(Grammar and usage)**

Answer #64: (B)

The correct answer is B. When items in a series include commas, a semicolon must separate the items. The other choices include punctuation errors. Answer A, for instance, lacks a semicolon between "Ohio" and "Seattle." Answer C incorrectly uses semicolons to separate the city and state or city and country. Answer D has none of the necessary semicolons. **(Punctuation)**

65. **(A)** NO CHANGE
(B) denial then
(C) denial. Then
(D) denial and then

66. **(A)** NO CHANGE
(B) the driving in ways I don't like.
(C) itty-bitty mistakes.
(D) the smallest of infractions.

65. (A) (B) (C) (D)

66. (A) (B) (C) (D)

Answer #65: Ⓒ

The correct answer is C. Answer A includes a comma splice because there is only a comma to connect the two independent clauses. Answer B is a run-on or fused sentence because it does not include any proper punctuation or conjunction to connect the clauses. Answer D needs a comma after "denial" to comply with the rule that a comma and a coordinate conjunction can join independent clauses. **(Sentence structure)**

Answer #66: Ⓓ

The correct answer is D. The language in Answer A is too informal or colloquial. Answer B is vague. Answer C is similarly informal or colloquial. Only D suits the style of this passage. **(Style)**

67. The author wants to add a topic sentence to the second paragraph. The best choice would be:

(A) I find that I like to remember my past in Los Angeles.
(B) The anger phase becomes transformed into sentimentality.
(C) After having been angry, it becomes easier to adjust to the idea of moving.
(D) No matter how often I do it, I still dislike leaving home.

68. **(A)** NO CHANGE
(B) with who I have always kept in touch.
(C) I have always kept in touch with him.
(D) I have always with him kept in touch.

---

67. Ⓐ Ⓑ Ⓒ Ⓓ

68. Ⓐ Ⓑ Ⓒ Ⓓ

Answer #67: (B)

The correct answer is B. It provides effective transition to connect the main idea of paragraph 1 to that of paragraph 2. Answer A is pertinent to the ideas in paragraph 2, but it does not afford any transition. Answer C oversimplifies the process being described. Answer D is a more effective topic sentence for paragraph 1. **(Organization)**

Answer #68: (A)

The correct answer is A. Answer B incorrectly uses "who," the nominative case pronoun, as the object of the preposition "with." Answer C creates a comma splice, since there is no conjunction to accompany the comma connecting the two independent clauses. Answer D also creates a comma splice with an especially awkward second clause. **(Grammar and usage)**

69. The author wants to add the word "Eventually" to the first sentence of paragraph 3. The author should do so because:

(A) The sentence is too short.
(B) It adds to the sentence's coherence.
(C) It provides a transition from paragraph 2 to paragraph 3.
(D) It provides necessary information without which the sentence doesn't make sense.

70. **(A)** NO CHANGE
(B) phone calls and I leave a change of address notice at the post office, and sign
(C) phone calls, leave a change of address notice at the post office, and sign
(D) phone calls leave a change of address notice at the post office and sign

69. (A) (B) (C) (D)

70. (A) (B) (C) (D)

Answer #69: Ⓒ

The correct answer is C. It helps to develop the flow of ideas more smoothly. The other choices are not accurate descriptions of the word's function. The length of the sentence is unimportant (Answer A). "Eventually" does not add to the sentence's coherence (Answer B). "Eventually" does not provide necessary information without which the sentence does not make sense (Answer D). **(Strategy)**

Answer #70: Ⓒ

The correct answer is C. Answer A shifts from third to second person because "Leave" has an understood "you" as its subject. Answer B is a wordy sentence that has problems with a lack of parallelism (Two independent clauses: "I make . . ." and "I leave . . ." are not followed by a parallel expression: "and sign," which should be "I sign."). Answer D incorrectly omits commas between items in a series. **(Sentence structure)**

71. **(A)** NO CHANGE
(B) parent's phone number:
(C) parents phone numbers:
(D) parents' phone number.

72. **(A)** NO CHANGE
(B) give
(C) gave
(D) had given

71. (A) (B) (C) (D)

72. (A) (B) (C) (D)

Answer #71: Ⓓ

The correct answer is D. "Parents'" is the plural possessive form. Answer A contains no apostrophe to show possession for "parents." Answer B offers the singular possessive form. Answer C contains no apostrophe to show possession, offering instead the plural of "number." **(Grammar and usage)**

Answer #72: Ⓑ

The correct answer is B to maintain use of present tense. Answer A shifts to the present perfect tense. Answer C changes to past tense. Answer D shifts to past perfect tense. Aim to maintain a consistency in tenses when you write unless there is a need to use a different tense. Review the process by which different tenses are formed. Here is an example: present—walk, past—walked (adding -ed to the present tense form typically forms the past tense), future—will walk, present perfect—has or have walked (the perfect tenses are based on the past participle form of the verb), past perfect—had walked, and future perfect—will have walked. **(Grammar and usage)**

73. The writer wants to add a sentence to paragraph 3: "All of these actions seem like a complicated game I have played many times." The best place to do so is:

(A) After sentence 1
(B) After sentence 3
(C) After sentence 6
(D) After sentence 8

74. This passage describes a:

(A) scene
(B) contrast
(C) process
(D) character

73. (A) (B) (C) (D)

74. (A) (B) (C) (D)

Answer #73: Ⓓ

The correct answer is D. Used in this fashion, the added sentence will summarize and afford transition. Placing the new sentence after sentence 1 is awkward because the use of "these" implies an antecedent (a word to which the pronoun refers) that does not exist. Placing the new sentence after sentences 3 or 6 is also inappropriate because the flow of ideas will be interrupted. **(Organization)**

Answer #74: Ⓒ

The correct answer is C. The passage describes steps in the process of leaving. Writing about a scene (Answer A) is usually descriptive. Writing a contrast (Answer B) involves two different topics, but this passage offers only one. This passage does not emphasize character (Answer D) although some characters are mentioned. **(Strategy)**

75. **(A)** NO CHANGE
(B) Trying to ignore the sadness of good-byes; I promise to write to them often.
(C) Trying to ignore the sadness of good-byes: I promise to write to them often.
(D) Trying to ignore the sadness of good-byes I promise to write to them often.

Answer #75: Ⓐ

The correct answer is A. The comma is correctly placed after an introductory participial phrase. Answers B and C incorrectly place a semicolon and a colon, respectively, after the participial phrase. Answer D does not include the needed punctuation after the participial phrase. The participle form of a verb is usually formed by adding -ed or -ing to the present tense form of the verb. Participles function like adjectives; they can follow or precede the word modified. An introductory participial phrase (the participle plus any modifiers or objects) is followed by comma. **(Grammar and usage)**

TEST 2

DIRECTIONS: In the five passages that follow, certain words and phrases are underlined and numbered. Following the passage, you will find alternatives for each underlined part. You are to choose the one that best expresses the idea, makes the statement appropriate for standard written English, or is worded most consistently with the style and tone of the passage as a whole. If you think the original version is best, choose "NO CHANGE."

Passage 1

[1]

Technology seems to have lessened the impact of some experiences. Because a century ago a trip across the United States might have been by railroad or wagon <u>and could take weeks or months, the travelers</u> (1) of a century ago experienced the immensity of the continent. Now the same trip takes several hours in <u>an airplane and one can</u> (2) barely get a night's sleep or a nap during the journey. <u>But, technology has also provided situations. That by</u> (3) their very newness and contrast to <u>an older experience has</u> (4) the power to change our view of our world.

[2]

In space, for example, perceptions are forced out of familiar patterns. From Earth's orbit, our planet can be seen as a <u>finite globe and it can be orbited</u> (5) in an hour and a half. The borders that people have fought over cannot be seen. <u>One sees rivers, forests, plains, and mountains,</u> (6) <u>but you cannot see</u> (7) which have run reddest with blood.

[3]

[1] One astronaut likened the view of Earth from the moon to seeing a Christmas ornament, large perhaps, but beautiful and fragile; not to be fought over lest it be broken. [2] From the moon, a picture was taken of Earth resting <u>on an astronauts</u> (8) upraised palm. [3] True, this was a trick of photography; but what a trick! [4] Earth was reduced to no more than a ball in a man's hand, but one views that ball while standing on the large, <u>solid Earth that we have known from birth.</u> (9)

[4]

<u>Still, technology can take our viewpoint even further</u> (12) to the point where the experience of humanity's uniqueness is threatened. No signs of other intelligences have yet been found. But for those who look at the night sky and see not stars but far off suns, who look at <u>our son</u> (13) and see a star that an alien scientist may even now be measuring for wobbles to indicate the presence of planets, our Earth is both the center of the universe and a small satellite of an average star.

1. **(A)** NO CHANGE
   (B) and could take weeks or months the travelers
   (C) and could take weeks, or months, the travelers
   (D) and could take weeks, or months the travelers

2. **(A)** NO CHANGE.
   (B) in an airplane, and one can
   (C) in an airplane and one can't
   (D) in an airplane, and one can't

1. (A) (B) (C) (D)

2. (A) (B) (C) (D)

Answer #1: Ⓐ

The correct answer is A. A comma is required after "months" to set off the introductory adverb clause. Answer B omits the necessary punctuation. Answer C incorrectly includes a comma to separate the parts of a compound direct object. In Answer D the comma is also misplaced between the parts of the compound direct object. **(Punctuation)**

Answer #2: Ⓑ

The correct answer is B. A comma is necessary to separate two independent clauses joined by a coordinate conjunction, such as "and." Answer A does not include this required comma. Both Answer C and Answer D contain usage errors called "double negatives." This kind of error occurs when you use two negative forms at the same time. In addition to "not," "scarcely" and " hardly" are negative forms. Omit "not" from the sentence or eliminate the negative adverb to avoid this kind of mistake in your writing. **(Sentence structure)**

3. **(A)** NO CHANGE
(B) But technology has also provided situations, that by
(C) But technology has also provided situations. That by
(D) But technology has also provided situations that by

4. **(A)** NO CHANGE
(B) an older experience have
(C) older experiences have
(D) older experiences has

3. Ⓐ Ⓑ Ⓒ Ⓓ

4. Ⓐ Ⓑ Ⓒ Ⓓ

Answer #3: (D)

The correct answer is D. Answers A and C contain sentence fragments; "But technology has also provided situations" cannot stand alone as a complete thought. Answer B contains an unnecessary comma to set off a restrictive or essential clause. Answer D is the best choice because it correctly combines the sentence fragment and the sentence that follows to create a complete sentence. **(Sentence structure)**

Answer #4: (C)

The correct answer is C. Answer C changes "experience" to "experiences," which is the correct form because the author refers to a number of previous experiences, not just one. Answer A is incorrect because it includes a subject-verb agreement mistake. "That" is a plural pronoun because its antecedent is "situations." Although Answer B corrects the subject-verb agreement problem, it does not address another error. "Experience" should be plural because the writer is discussing "situations." Answer D fails to correct the subject-verb agreement error. **(Grammar and usage)**

5. **(A)** NO CHANGE
(B) finite globe, and it can be orbited
(C) finite globe, it can be orbited
(D) finite globe it can be orbited

6. **(A)** NO CHANGE
(B) rivers, forests, plains and mountains,
(C) rivers forests plains, and mountains,
(D) rivers forests plains and mountains,

5. (A) (B) (C) (D)

6. (A) (B) (C) (D)

Answer #5: 

The correct answer is B. Two independent clauses connected by a coordinate conjunction such as "and" should be separated by a comma. Answer A fails to include a comma. Answer C creates a comma splice by joining the two independent clauses with only a comma. Answer D creates a run-on or fused sentence because no conjunction or appropriate punctuation joins the clauses. **(Sentence structure)**

Answer #6: (A)

The correct answer is A. Items in a series must be separated by commas. A comma should be placed between the final item and "and." The other answers omit necessary commas. **(Punctuation)**

7. **(A)** NO CHANGE
(B) but they cannot see
(C) but one cannot see
(D) but he cannot see

8. **(A)** NO CHANGE
(B) on a astronauts
(C) on an astronauts'
(D) on an astronaut's

7. (A) (B) (C) (D)

8. (A) (B) (C) (D)

Answer #7: Ⓒ

The correct answer is C. Maintain the person (first, second, or third) or number (singular or plural) of pronouns within a sentence. Answer A shifts to second person ("you"). Answer B changes from a singular ("you") to plural pronoun ("they"). Answer D changes from a third person neutral pronoun ("it") to a masculine gender ("he"). **(Style)**

Answer #8: Ⓓ

The correct answer is D. "Astronaut's" is the singular possessive form. Answer A has no apostrophe and does not show possession. Answer B includes a usage error of "a" before a word that begins with a vowel. Answer C presents the plural possessive form ("astronauts' "). **(Punctuation)**

9. **(A)** NO CHANGE
(B) solid Earth that one has known from birth.
(C) solid Earth we have been living on ever since the very first day that we were born.
(D) solid Earth on which we were born.

10. The author wishes to add the word "merely" to the third sentence in paragraph 3. The best place to add the word is:

(A) After the word "True."
(B) After the word "was."
(C) After the word "but."
(D) After the second time the word "a" appears in the sentence.

---

9. (A) (B) (C) (D)

10. (A) (B) (C) (D)

Answer #9: (B)

The correct answer is B. This choice maintains the third-person perspective established earlier in the passage. Answer A shifts from third person ("one") to first person ("we"). Answer C is wordy. Answer D also shifts from third person ("one") to first person ("we"). **(Style)**

Answer #10: (B)

The correct answer is B. Place adverbs as closely as possible to the word modified. "Merely" here modifies "was." The other answers place "merely" in illogical places. Try each answer to determine the best placement. **(Sentence structure)**

11. The author wants to add an opening sentence to paragraph 3. The best choice would be:

(A) Traveling farther out, Earth becomes smaller.
(B) As one travels farther out, Earth becomes smaller.
(C) Astronauts have looked at the Earth while they were on the moon.
(D) However, Mars has also been known as the Red Planet.

12. **(A)** NO CHANGE
(B) However, technology can take our viewpoint further
(C) Technology can take our viewpoint even further
(D) Technology can take our viewpoint further than that

11. (A) (B) (C) (D)

12. (A) (B) (C) (D)

Answer #11: Ⓑ

The correct answer is B. Answer A sets up a dangling modifier (Was the earth "traveling farther out"?). Because it contains information about astronauts and their view of the Earth, Answer C could function within paragraph 3, but it does not provide effective transition. Answer D is not relevant to the subject. Mars is not mentioned in paragraph 3. **(Strategy)**

Answer #12: Ⓒ

The correct answer is C. Answer A offers only weak transition ("Still"). Answer B sets up a contrast ("However") rather than addition; Answer D is wordy and includes a pronoun ("that") for which there is no clear antecedent. (To what does "that" refer?) **(Strategy)**

13. **(A)** NO CHANGE
(B) our sun
(C) are son
(D) our Son

14. The author wants to add the following sentence to the passage: "Suddenly, all that was familiar is strange." The best place to add it is:

(A) As the first sentence of paragraph 1.
(B) As the last sentence of paragraph 2.
(C) As the first sentence of paragraph 4.
(D) As the last sentence of paragraph 4.

13. Ⓐ Ⓑ Ⓒ Ⓓ

14. Ⓐ Ⓑ Ⓒ Ⓓ

Answer #13: (B)

The correct answer is B. The other answers offer the homonym "son." Be sure to check spelling carefully. **(Style)**

Answer #14: (D)

The correct answer is D. The sentence provides a summary of the entire passage. The other answers weaken the opening generalization for the entire passage (Answer A) or interrupt the flow of ideas (Answers B and C). **(Organization)**

15. The author's intention in this passage is best stated as:

(A) describing the view of Earth from the moon.
(B) contrasting the past and the present.
(C) exemplifying an effect of technology.
(D) analyzing means of transportation.

Answer #15: Ⓒ

The correct answer is C. Answer A is too limited. Answers B and D do not deal with the main idea of the passage. **(Organization)**

Passage 2

[1]

[1] One of the most famous works by the Belgian Surrealist Rene Magritte *The Treachery of Images* was painted (16) in 1929. [2] (17) It is a gouache, (an opaque watercolor painting) (18) of an ordinary brown tobacco pipe with a black pipestem on a beige background. [3] Beneath the pipe, in black painted handwriting, appear French words, which, translated, read "This Is Not A Pipe." [4] But on further reflection, one realizes that this is not a pipe. [5] It is a painting of a pipe, an image of a pipe, but it is not the pipe itself.

[2]

[1] Many of Magritte's works suggest that painting creates only (20) illusions. Yet the style is as realistic as the photograph in a glossy magazine advertisement. [2] Sometimes the works do this by creating impossible realities. [3] In *The Dominion of Light, II*, an oil painting, an ordinary street of small houses, some hidden by trees, is in darkness. [4] One street lamp illuminates the center house. Which is dark. (21) [5] The houses to its (22) immediate left and right have lighted windows, and the houses at the far edges of the painting are hidden by trees, whose trunks cannot be seen distinctly because of the darkness. [6] Above the trees and houses however the sky is filled with puffy white clouds (23) against a background colored the bright azure blue of a spring day.

[3]

His art also calls attention to themselves as false reality by the use
25
of frames and windows. In one painting, inside the frame is a painting of a frame surrounding a painting! The effect is so realistic that one must approach the painting closely to realized the second frame is
26
painted on a flat canvas. It is not an additional three-dimensional wooden frame. In another painting, the viewer seems to be looking through an open window at a view above some rooftops. Floating
27
above the rooftops, a loaf of bread and an empty wineglass are seen.
27
The viewer looks through a broken window at a sunset in "Evening
28
Falls." In the room beneath the broken window are jagged pieces of
28
glass on which appear the same sunset as one sees through the window.

[4]

Are these paintings making a profound statement about illusion and reality? Are they commenting on the nature of art? Right on! But it
29
is also undeniable that the paintings are funny; they make the viewer smile because of their incongruities. And it cannot be doubted that
30
Magritte had a sense of humor. In 1952, he did a pencil drawing of a pipe. Like the earlier gouache, it was titled *The Treachery of Images.* Beneath the pipe, he wrote, "This is still not a pipe."

16. **(A)** NO CHANGE
(B) Rene Magritte, *The Treachery of Images* was painted
(C) Rene Magritte, *The Treachery of Images*, was painted
(D) Rene Magritte *The Treachery of Images*, was painted

17. **(A)** NO CHANGE
(B) in 1929, it is
(C) in 1929. It was
(D) in 1929, it was

---

16. (A) (B) (C) (D)

17. (A) (B) (C) (D)

Answer #16: Ⓒ

The correct answer is C. The title of the painting is an appositive, which should be set off from the text by commas. Answer A omits necessary commas. Answer B includes one comma after "Magritte" but fails to set the appositive off by a concluding comma after "*Images.*" Answer D omits a comma after "Magritte." **(Punctuation)**

Answer #17: Ⓐ

The correct answer is A. Answer B creates a comma splice by connecting the independent clauses with a comma. Answer C shifts from present to past tense. Answer D both creates a comma splice and shifts tenses. **(Sentence structure)**

18. **(A)** NO CHANGE
(B) gouache, (an opaque watercolor painting),
(C) gouache (an opaque watercolor painting),
(D) gouaches (an opaque watercolor painting)

19. The author wishes to add the following sentence to paragraph 1: "A viewer's first reaction is 'But of course it's a pipe. It's not an automobile; it's not a tree; it's not a cow'." The best place to add this sentence is:

(A) After sentence 1
(B) After sentence 2
(C) After sentence 3
(D) After sentence 4

18. (A) (B) (C) (D)

19. (A) (B) (C) (D)

Answer #18: Ⓓ

The correct answer is D. When parenthetical material is used, commas are not needed. If "an opaque watercolor painting" had not been placed within parentheses, the phrase could have been set off by commas. Answer A is wrong because it includes an unnecessary comma after "goache." Answer B is incorrect because it includes both parentheses and commas. Answer C needlessly includes a comma after the closing parentheses. Use either parentheses or commas. **(Punctuation)**

Answer #19: Ⓒ

The correct answer is C. This choice after the third sentence is the best selection because this additional sentence responds to a statement on Magritte's painting. Answer A is wrong because the reader does not yet know the title of the painting. Answer B seems pointless, since the reader does not understand the contrast set up by "but." Answer D offers an illogical placement. **(Organization)**

20. **(A)** NO CHANGE
(B) only creates
(C) create only
(D) only create

21. **(A)** NO CHANGE
(B) center house which is dark.
(C) center house; which is dark.
(D) center house, which is dark.

20. Ⓐ Ⓑ Ⓒ Ⓓ

21. Ⓐ Ⓑ Ⓒ Ⓓ

Answer #20: (B)

The correct answer is B. The modifier "only" is misplaced in Answer A, where it modifies "creates" (as opposed, for instance, to "depicts"), not "illusions." Answer C sets up an error in subject-verb agreement. Answer D repeats the error made in A, and it also contains an error in subject-verb agreement. Watch out for sentences that include modifiers such as "only" to make sure that the placement of the modifier is accurate. **(Sentence structure)**

Answer #21: (D)

The correct answer is D. This choice eliminates the sentence fragment and correctly attaches it to the previous sentence as a nonrestrictive adjective clause. Answer A presents a sentence fragment because "Which is dark" cannot stand alone as a complete thought. Answers B and C create punctuation errors. The clause "which is dark" is a nonrestrictive clause, one that is not essential to the meaning of the sentence. Answer B needs a comma after "house"; Answer C incorrectly offers a semicolon to connect a dependent clause to an independent clause. **(Sentence structure)**

22. **(A)** NO CHANGE
(B) houses to it's
(C) houses to its'
(D) houses, to its

23. **(A)** NO CHANGE
(B) Above the tress and houses; however the sky is filled with puffy white clouds
(C) Above the trees and houses, however, the sky is filled with puffy white clouds
(D) Above the trees and houses, however; the sky is filled with puffy white clouds,

22. (A) (B) (C) (D)

23. (A) (B) (C) (D)

Answer #22: Ⓐ

The correct answer is A. The possessive form of the third person singular neutral pronoun "it" is "its." Apostrophes are not used to show possession in pronouns. In Answer B "it's" is a contraction for "it is." Answer C misuses an apostrophe to create an incorrect form of "it." Answer D includes an unnecessary comma. **(Punctuation)**

Answer #23: Ⓒ

The correct answer is C. An introductory prepositional phrase of at least four words should be set off by a comma. Answer A does not include a comma. Answer B incorrectly places a semicolon after the prepositional phrase. Answer D is wrong because it misplaces a semicolon after "however," which is used as a transition word in this sentence rather than as a conjunctive adverb. **(Punctuation)**

24. The author wishes to add the words "For example" to the beginning of paragraph 3. The best reason to do so is:

(A) to make the paragraph longer.
(B) to improve coherence.
(C) to be more specific.
(D) to unify the paragraph.

25. **(A)** NO CHANGE
(B) art also call attention to themselves
(C) art also call attention to itself
(D) art also calls attention to itself

---

24. (A) (B) (C) (D)

25. (A) (B) (C) (D)

Answer #24: Ⓒ

The correct answer is C. "For example" sets up a specific instance to illustrate the idea of illusion. Answer A is not a sound reason; the length of a paragraph is not necessarily a sign of quality. Neither Answer B nor D is relevant because the paragraph does not suffer problems with coherence or unity. Coherence in writing refers to logic development while unity is concerned with whether every sentence pertains to the main idea. **(Strategy)**

Answer #25: Ⓓ

The correct answer is D. "Art" is singular and therefore requires the singular form of the verb "calls" and the singular pronoun "itself." Answer A includes an agreement error between "art" and "themselves." Answer B has a subject-verb agreement error: "art . . . call." Answer C corrects the pronoun-antecedent error but still includes the subject-verb error. **(Grammar and usage)**

26. **(A)** NO CHANGE
(B) to realize
(C) in realizing
(D) while realizing

27. **(A)** NO CHANGE
(B) Floating above the rooftops, the viewer sees a loaf of bread and an empty wineglass.
(C) Floating above the rooftops are pictured a loaf of bread and an empty wineglass.
(D) Floating above the rooftops, we find a loaf of bread and an empty wineglass.

Answer #26: (B)

The correct answer is B. The infinitive form (to + verb) is needed to complete the sentence. Answer A includes an incorrect verb form; to form a perfect infinitive, you must also include an auxiliary such as "have." Answer C offers a prepositional phrase with a gerund as the object; the phrase is correct, but it is not used correctly to tell why "one must approach the painting closely." Answer D creates an unnecessary elliptical adverb clause. "Elliptical" refers to any construction in which words have been omitted but are understood. Here "while realizing" is a shortened form of "while (someone) is realizing." The subject of this clause is unknown. **(Grammar and usage)**

Answer #27: (A)

The correct answer is A. Answers B and D present dangling modifiers. Answer B offers the viewer "floating above the rooftop," while in D "we" are "[f]loating above the rooftops." Answer C rearranges and changes the verb without actually correcting any error. **(Sentence structure)**

28. **(A)** NO CHANGE
(B) "Evening falls".
(C) "Evening Falls."
(D) *Evening falls.*

29. **(A)** NO CHANGE
(B) Maybe yes, maybe no.
(C) Certainly, that is possible.
(D) It perhaps may be argued that such is the case.

28. (A) (B) (C) (D)

29. (A) (B) (C) (D)

Answer #28: Ⓓ

The correct answer is D. The title of the painting should be italicized or underlined. The other answers incorrectly use quotation marks. **(Punctuation)**

Answer #29: Ⓒ

The correct answer is C. Answer A is slang, the kind of language we use in casual conversation with our friends. Answer B is needlessly ambivalent. Answer D is pretentious and wordy; the language is too stiff to be appropriate for the rest of the passage. **(Style)**

30. **(A)** NO CHANGE
(B) incongruities, and it cannot be doubted
(C) incongruities it cannot be doubted
(D) incongruities but it cannot be doubted

Answer #30: (B)

The correct answer is B. Answer A includes a sentence fragment because it begins with a coordinate conjunction ("And it cannot . . ."). Answer C is a run-on or fused sentence because two independent clauses are joined without proper punctuation or conjunction. Answer D omits the necessary comma after "incongruities" and changes the meaning of the sentence by using "but" to show a contrast. **(Sentence structure)**

Passage 3

[1]

We take our smoothly paved interstate highways and streets for granted as products of technology and engineering. They are made of concrete, a building material <u>apprised of cement,</u> (31) sand or gravel, and water. The cement in concrete has a long history. The Egyptians burned chips from the Great Pyramid and used the resulting ash as mortar. The Romans made a cement out of volcanic <u>ash, and which they turned</u> (32) into concrete by mixing it with water, lime, and rock. <u>Today, concrete mix containing sand is used for smooth applications; gravel mix is used where a stronger concrete is required.</u> (33) They used cement in the Great Aqueduct, which supplied Ancient Rome with drinking water, as well as in the Coliseum and the Baths of Caracalla.

[2]

<u>[1] During Europe's Dark Ages, the art</u> (34) of cement making was lost. It was rediscovered <u>by John Smeaton, in 1756, he had been hired</u> (35) to rebuild a burned lighthouse off the coast of <u>Plymouth England.</u> (36) [2] He experimented and found that he could make cement with volcanic ash he had purchased at a local warehouse <u>where it had been imported</u> (37) from Italy. [3] He combined the ash with clay and limestone, and the result was cement. [4] <u>The Eddystone Lighthouse which he rebuilt was later razed and replaced by a taller tower.</u> (38)

[3]

Consequently, seventy-five years later, another British inventor,
39
Joseph Aspdin, patented a new form of cement. He swept up dust from highways where wagon wheels had crushed the limestone paving into dust. He mixed the dust with red clay, cooked it to a cinder, and pulverized that into a powder. Which he mixed with water. He found
40
his mixture surprisingly like the stone quarried on the Isle of Portland, so he named his product Portland Cement.

[4]

Cement was first patented in the United States in 1871 by David O. Saylor. He too called his product Portland Cement, but it was made
41
with American materials. By the beginning of the twentieth century, there was sixteen manufacturing plants producing American Portland
42
Cement.

[5]

The strength of concrete depends on the amount of cement in the mix. A sixty-pound bag of concrete mix that has only seven pounds of cement in it may be okay for sinking a fence post. But for
43
applications where strong concrete is needful, there should be at least
44
fourteen pounds of cement in a sixty pound bag of concrete mix.

31. **(A)** NO CHANGE
(B) incorporated by
(C) compromised of
(D) composed of

32. **(A)** NO CHANGE
(B) ash, and they turned
(C) ash, which they turned
(D) ash, but it was turned

31. (A) (B) (C) (D)

32. (A) (B) (C) (D)

Answer #31: Ⓓ

The correct answer is D. "Composed of" means "made up of." In Answer A "apprised" means "kept informed." Answer B is illogical because "incorporate" means "to form into one body by outside forces" (not by the ingredients themselves). Answer C also offers an inappropriate choice; "compromised" means "came to an agreement." **(Style)**

Answer #32: Ⓒ

The correct answer is C. Answer A includes an unnecessary "and." Answer B is incorrect because there is no direct object for "turned." Answer D is incorrect because "but" sets up an illogical contrast. **(Sentence structure)**

33. This sentence should be removed from the paragraph because:

(A) it contains incorrect punctuation.
(B) it makes the paragraph too long.
(C) it interrupts the chronological structure.
(D) it does not contain interesting information.

34. **(A)** NO CHANGE
(B) During Europe's Dark Ages the art
(C) During Europes Dark Ages, the art
(D) During Europes Dark Ages the art

---

33. Ⓐ Ⓑ Ⓒ Ⓓ

34. Ⓐ Ⓑ Ⓒ Ⓓ

Answer #33: Ⓒ

The correct answer is C. The sentence interrupts the unity of the paragraph by shifting to the present. The other sentences in the paragraph offer a discussion of cement in the past, not the present. **(Organization)**

Answer #34: Ⓐ

The correct answer is A. An introductory prepositional phrase is set off by a comma; the possessive form of "Europe" is formed by adding an apostrophe -s to "Europe." Answer B omits the needed comma. Answer C omits the needed apostrophe. Answer D lacks both the apostrophe and the comma. **(Punctuation)**

35. **(A)** NO CHANGE
(B) John Smeaton in 1756, he had been hired
(C) John Smeaton in 1756 he had been hired
(D) John Smeaton in 1756; he had been hired

36. **(A)** NO CHANGE
(B) Plymouth, England.
(C) Plymouth in England
(D) Plymouth, in England,

35. (A) (B) (C) (D)

36. (A) (B) (C) (D)

Answer #35: Ⓓ

The correct answer is D. The semicolon in this choice correctly joins the two independent clauses. Answers A and B create comma splices when a comma is incorrectly used to joined two independent clauses. Answer C creates a fused or run-on sentence in which there is no appropriate punctuation to join the independent clauses. **(Sentence structure)**

Answer #36: Ⓑ

The correct answer is B. A comma should separate the name of a city and a country. Answer A has no comma between Plymouth and England. Answers C and D are incorrect because the lighthouse is "off the coast" and cannot logically be "in England." Be sure to read the choices carefully. **(Punctuation)**

37. **(A)** NO CHANGE
(B) that had imported it from
(C) which had been imported
(D) the ash had been imported from

38. The author is thinking of deleting this sentence from the passage.

(A) It should not be deleted because it contributes to the paragraph's unity.
(B) It should not be deleted because the reader needs to know the name of the lighthouse.
(C) It should be deleted because it is not related to the history of cement.
(D) It should be deleted because the paragraph is sufficiently long without it.

37. (A) (B) (C) (D)

38. (A) (B) (C) (D)

Answer #37: (B)

The correct answer is B. Answer A is wordy and ambiguous; the passive voice verb "had been imported" is confusing. Answer C creates a misplaced modifier; with this choice the warehouse "had been imported from Italy." Answer D creates a run-on or fused sentence because it lacks the necessary punctuation and/or conjunction to connect the clauses. **(Style)**

Answer #38: (C)

The correct answer is C. The sentence is not relevant to the history of cement. Answer A is incorrect because this sentence weakens the paragraph's unity. Answer B offers irrelevant information. Answer D offers an illogical choice. The length of the paragraph is not the issue here. **(Organization)**

39. **(A)** NO CHANGE
(B) Thus seventy-five
(C) Next, seventy-five
(D) About seventy-five

40. **(A)** NO CHANGE
(B) powder, which he mixed.
(C) powder; which he mixed.
(D) powder—which he mixed.

---

39. (A) (B) (C) (D)

40. (A) (B) (C) (D)

Answer #39: (D)

The correct answer is D. The other answers do not provide appropriate transition between paragraphs. "Consequently" means "following this." "Thus" shows a cause-effect relationship that does not exist here. "Next" implies an event that occurs much sooner than seventy-five years. "About seventy-five" in Answer D most effectively accounts for the shift in time. **(Strategy)**

Answer #40: (B)

The correct answer is B. Answer A is a sentence fragment. Answer C incorrectly uses a semicolon to connect the dependent clause to the main clause. Answer D incorrectly relies on a hyphen to connect the clauses. Hyphens are used to divide words or to attach certain prefixes, not to connect clauses. **(Sentence structure)**

41. **(A)** NO CHANGE
(B) Portland Cement but it was made
(C) Portland Cement which it was made
(D) Portland Cement, and it was made

42. **(A)** NO CHANGE
(B) there were sixteen
(C) there is sixteen
(D) there are sixteen

41. (A) (B) (C) (D)

42. (A) (B) (C) (D)

Answer #41: (A)

The correct answer is A. Answer B is incorrect because a comma is needed after "Cement" before the coordinate conjunction. Answer C is incorrect because it contains two pronouns ("which" and "it") with the same antecedent ("Portland Cement"). Answer D is incorrect because "and" does not show the contrast needed. **(Sentence structure)**

Answer #42: (B)

The correct answer is B. The subject of the sentence is "plants," so the verb must be plural. Answer A includes a subject-verb agreement error. Answer C has the same subject-verb agreement error, and it changes to present tense. Answer D is incorrect because it has a tense shift. Watch out for sentences that begin with "There," for often the subject-verb order is reversed. "There" is never the subject of the sentence although it appears in the position most often held by a subject. "There" is an expletive; it has no function in this kind of sentence except to begin the sentence. **(Grammar and usage)**

43. **(A)** NO CHANGE
(B) cool
(C) utilitarian
(D) adequate

44. **(A)** NO CHANGE
(B) is needing
(C) is needed
(D) is kneaded

43. (A) (B) (C) (D)

44. (A) (B) (C) (D)

Answer #43: (D)

The correct answer is D. Answers A and B are slang expressions that are too informal to match the style of the rest of the passage. Although "utilitarian" in Answer C means "useful," the language in this choice does not match the rest of the passage either. **(Style)**

Answer #44: (C)

The correct answer is C. Answers A and B are awkward uses of passive voice. Answer D offers a homonym. Watch the spelling carefully. **(Grammar and usage)**

45. The best title for this selection would be:

(A) Hard As a Rock
(B) Speaking Concretely
(C) The Story of Cement
(D) A History of Building Materials

Answer #45: Ⓒ

The correct answer is C. Answer A has little relevance to the passage; the hardness of cement is never mentioned. Answer B is a clever pun, but it serves little purpose to explain the main idea of the passage. Answer D is too broad; the passage deals only with the history of cement. **(Strategy)**

Passage 4

[1]

[1] On my planet, many scholars focus their attention on the study of the religions of the creatures of the universe. [2] Although the creatures and their worlds are diverse, they have discovered (47) that many of these religions practice similar rituals. [3] To gain identification with a deity by symbolically consuming its flesh is a common religious practice. [4] Archaeologists theorize that this practice evolved from primitive rituals involving cannibalism. One ate the flesh of enemies to show one's triumph over them and to gain its strength symbolically. (48)

[2]

In one ritual on Earth, which takes place in buildings called churches, (49) bread and wine symbolically represent the flesh and blood of a deity. Another ritual of the same type and similar to the ritual that occurs in churches (50) takes place at various sites, each of which is known as a Temple of the Golden Arches. At this temple, the most sacred of the prayed-for substances is known as the Big Mac; it is the symbolic flesh (51) of the temple's chief deity.

[3]

[1] Arriving in a family group, the ritual begins. (52) [2] Upon entering the temple, the children and one of the adults (if two adults are present) (53) seat themselves at a table, while the other adult acts as chief worship-

per. [3] The worshipper approaches the altar, behind which stand several temple servants. [4] The servant begins the ritual by asking what the worshipper is praying for. [5] The words of each server is identical. [6] It is believed that the prayed-for substances are blessed by the chief deity of the Temple. [7] This deity rarely appears personally, yet his image is prominent in the temple's decorations. [8] Although he seems to be a human like the other inhabitants of the planet, he has a nose unlike theirs, as it is a large red sphere.

54 (words of each server is identical.)
55 (It is believed that the prayed-for substances are)

[4]

In order to receive the prayed-for substances, the worshipper must present paper and metal tokens to the server. Who then gives the substances to the worshipper. They are taken back to the family group and consumed. It is interesting to note that in this religion, prayer by itself is not sufficient to gain the gods gifts, but tokens must be given to receive the sacred substances. The inhabitants of Earth perform labor to earn these tokens, and the tokens are used to provide the inhabitants with physical necessities. Thus, their use in a religious ceremony may appear strange. Because this culture has a complex economical structure, however, it may be expected that even spiritual transactions have a material component.

58 (to the server. Who then gives)
59 (gods gifts,)
60 (economical structure,)

46. The writer is thinking of omitting sentences 1 and 2 of paragraph 1. The writer should not do so because:

(A) the paragraph would then be too short.
(B) these sentences are needed to set up the imaginary perspective of the passage.
(C) they explain that the universe is made up of creatures on many planets.
(D) the sentences provide unity for the paragraph.

47. **(A)** NO CHANGE
(B) it has been discovered that
(C) it has been discovered by our scientists
(D) our scientists have discovered

46. (A) (B) (C) (D)

47. (A) (B) (C) (D)

Answer #46: (B)

The correct answer is B. This choice with its "creatures of the universe" suggests an imaginary approach. Answer A does not present a legitimate reason because the length of the paragraph is not the issue. Answer C is not relevant. Answer D is not an accurate description of the task performed by these sentences. **(Organization)**

Answer #47: (D)

The correct answer is D. Answer A has no clear antecedent (word to which the pronoun refers) for "they." Answer B uses the passive voice awkwardly. Answer C compounds the problem with passive voice by adding a prepositional phrase that could easily have been changed to effective active voice as Answer D does. **(Sentence structure)**

48. **(A)** NO CHANGE
(B) to symbolically gain its strength.
(C) to gain their strength symbolically.
(D) to symbolically gain their strength.

49. **(A)** NO CHANGE
(B) buildings called Churches,
(C) buildings called churches
(D) buildings called Churches

48. (A) (B) (C) (D)

49. (A) (B) (C) (D)

Answer #48: (C)

The correct answer is C. This choice corrects the pronoun-antecedent error because "their" refers to "enemies." Answer A sets up this pronoun-antecedent agreement error. Answer B has this same error and also creates a split infinitive by insertion of an adverb between "to" and the verb "gain." Answer D corrects the pronoun error but still has a split infinitive. **(Grammar and usage)**

Answer #49: (A)

The correct answer is A. The nonrestrictive adjective clause is correctly set off by commas. No additional capitalization is needed because "churches" is a common noun. Answers C and D omit the comma needed at the end of the clause. **(Grammar and usage)**

50. **(A)** NO CHANGE
(B) The same type of ritual
(C) Another almost identical ritual
(D) A similar ritual

51. **(A)** NO CHANGE
(B) the Big Mac, it is the symbolic flesh of
(C) the Big Mac it is the symbolic flesh of
(D) the Big Mac its the symbolic flesh of

---

50. Ⓐ Ⓑ Ⓒ Ⓓ

51. Ⓐ Ⓑ Ⓒ Ⓓ

Answer #50: (D)

The correct answer is D. It provides effective transition with the use of "similar." The other answers are unnecessarily wordy. Look for the answer that most succinctly expresses the idea. **(Strategy)**

Answer #51: (A)

The correct answer is A. Answer B creates a comma splice by incorrectly connecting two independent clauses. Answer C creates a run-on or fused sentence because there is no appropriate punctuation to connect the clauses. Answer D likewise creates a run-on or fused sentence, and it contains a misspelling of the contraction "it's." "Its" is the possessive form of the pronoun "it." **(Sentence structure)**

52. **(A)** NO CHANGE
(B) Arriving in a family group, the beginning of the ritual occurs.
(C) The family arrives in a group of participants to this ritual.
(D) Participants in this ritual usually arrive in a family group.

53. **(A)** NO CHANGE
(B) one of the adults, (if two adults are present)
(C) one of the adults (if two adults are present),
(D) one of the adults, (if two adults are present),

52. Ⓐ Ⓑ Ⓒ Ⓓ

53. Ⓐ Ⓑ Ⓒ Ⓓ

Answer #52: (D)

The correct answer is D. Answers A and B create dangling participles. The participial phrase "arriving in a family group" should modify the noun closest to it. In Answer A did the "ritual" arrive in a family group? Answer B, another wrong choice, has "the beginning" arriving in a family group. Answer C is awkwardly phrased. Only Answer D expresses the idea logically and effectively. **(Sentence structure)**

Answer #53: (A)

The correct answer is A. The information is correctly set off by parentheses; no additional punctuation is necessary. Using both parentheses and commas is incorrect; use one or the other. Answers B and C incorrectly include a needless comma. Answer D wrongly has both parentheses and commas. **(Punctuation)**

54. **(A)** NO CHANGE
(B) words of each server are identical
(C) word of each server are identical
(D) words spoken by the servers is

55. **(A)** NO CHANGE
(B) I believe that the prayed-for substances
(C) The substances that are prayed for are
(D) The prayed-for substances are believed to be

---

54. Ⓐ Ⓑ Ⓒ Ⓓ

55. Ⓐ Ⓑ Ⓒ Ⓓ

Answer #54: (B)

The correct answer is B. This answer eliminates the subject-verb agreement error by offering "are" to agree with the plural subject "words." Answers C and D include errors in subject-verb agreement. In C "word . . . are" is incorrect; in D "words . . . is" is an error. **(Grammar and usage)**

Answer #55: (A)

The correct answer is A. This answer correctly uses the passive voice because it refers to all those who share the belief. Answer B presents an error because the speaker does not share this belief. Answer C presents the information as fact rather than belief. Answer D is wordy. **(Sentence structure)**

56. The writer wants to add the following sentence to paragraph 3: "His feet are larger than normal, and his hair's color does not appear naturally among the planet's inhabitants." The best place to add the sentence is:

(A) After sentence 3.
(B) After sentence 4.
(C) After sentence 7.
(D) After sentence 8.

57. The author is thinking of starting a new paragraph after sentence 5 of paragraph 3. This should be done because:

(A) the paragraph's subject changes from steps in the ritual to the deity.
(B) a paragraph is complete when it contains five sentences.
(C) sentences 6 through 8 contrast with sentences 1 through 5.
(D) this would improve the coherence of the passage.

56. (A) (B) (C) (D)

57. (A) (B) (C) (D)

Answer #56: (D)

The correct answer is D. Answers A and B are incorrect because "his feet" cannot logically refer those of the worshipper. Answer C is incorrect because sentence 7 does not sufficiently prepare the reader for the strange appearance of the deity. Sentence C sets up the contrast needed to add the sentence. **(Organization)**

Answer #57: (A)

The correct answer is A. This choice correctly identifies the shift in content. Answer B's assertion that a paragraph must contain five sentences is not true. The claims of Answer C are likewise false. Answer D offers only a vague reason. **(Strategy)**

58. **(A)** NO CHANGE
(B) to the server. Whom then gives
(C) to the server, who then gives
(D) to the serve, whom then gives

59. **(A)** NO CHANGE
(B) god's gift's
(C) gods' gifts
(D) god's gifts

58. (A) (B) (C) (D)

59. (A) (B) (C) (D)

Answer #58: Ⓒ

The correct answer is C. Answers A and B include sentence fragments, or incomplete sentences that cannot express a complete idea. Answer D includes an error in pronoun case by offering the objective case of "who" in the subject position; this answer also changes the spelling of "server" to "serve." Answer C correctly uses "who," and this choice includes a comma that sets off the adjective clause that modifies "server." Be sure to look carefully at all of the words in all of the choices. **(Sentence structure)**

Answer #59: Ⓓ

The correct answer is D. Answer A does not include the apostrophe to show possession for "god." The other answers use apostrophes incorrectly. Answer B correctly includes the possessive form of "god," but it incorrectly inserts an apostrophe in "gifts." Answer C presents the plural possessive form of "god." **(Punctuation)**

60. **(A)** NO CHANGE
(B) economy
(C) economically
(D) economic

Answer #60: Ⓓ

The correct answer is D. To modify "structure," "economic" is the most appropriate choice. Answer A has the wrong denotation; "thrifty" "structure" is not the intended meaning. Answer B is a noun and cannot modify "structure." Answer C is an adverb; thus it cannot modify "structure." Only an adjective can modify a noun. **(Style)**

Passage 5

[1]

Jack Roosevelt Robinson, better known as Jackie Robinson, was born in Cairo, Georgia, on January 31, 1919. Jackie's mother, Mallie, moved her four children abandoned by her husband (61) to Pasadena California in 1927. (62) Robinson, as most people know, grew up to become the first African-American to play major-league baseball. But perhaps only dedicated fans recall that Robinson was a superb and versatile athlete.

[2]

At Pasadena City College in 1938, Robinson quarterbacked his team to eleven consecutive victories. His basketball team won the junior college championship and he was named (63) to the all-California team. He played shortstop for the college's baseball team and was named the most (64) valuable player in southern California junior college baseball. Also he was on the track team too. (65) He broke his brother Mack's record for the broad jump among junior college athletes on May 8, 1938.

[3]

[1] In basketball, he twice led his division in scoring. [2] He won the broad jump championship. [3] But he dropped out of college a few credits shy of graduation to help his mother support the family.

[4] He lettered in baseball, basketball, football, and track at UCLA. [5] After working for a few years war broke out, (66) and Robinson joined the Army.

[4]

In 1946, Robinson is recruited (68) by Branch Ricky, the general manager and president of the Brooklyn Dodgers, to play for the club's Montreal minor-league team. During that season, Robertson led the league in batting with a .349 average, and he also had the league-leading fielding percentage of .985.

[5]

In 1947, he joined the Brooklyn Dodgers. In his first season, he was voted Rookie of the Year. He batted over .300 in the 1949 through 1954 seasons and led the National League in stolen bases in 1947 and 1949. He was the National League's Most Valuable Player in 1949, and he was named to the Hall of Fame in 1962. He was a member of the 1955 Dodgers. Who finally, after four previous attempts, (69) beat the hated New York Yankees to win their first World Series.

Baseball fans remembers Bobby Thompson's home run in a play-off that put the Giants, rather than the Dodgers, in the 1951 World Series. But it was Robinson's heroic fielding and hitting that had got (70) the Dodgers into the play-off. On the last day of the season,

the Dodgers and Philadelphia was tied for first place. In the final
71
play-off game, the score was tied in the twelfth inning. With a Philadelphia runner on third, Robinson made a diving catch for an out that ended the inning. In the top of the fourteenth inning, with two out, he slammed a pitch into the left field stands, which led to the Dodgers to a 9 to 8 victory.

[6]

Without Jackie Robinson's contributions, there wouldn't have
72
been Bobby Thompson's "Shot Heard 'Round The World." But without Robinson's courage in breaking the color line, there would have been no Willie Mays Hank Aaron or Darryl Strawberry.
73

61. **(A)** NO CHANGE
(B) Jackie's mother, Mallie, moved her four children, abandoned by her husband,
(C) Jackie's mother, Mallie, abandoned by her husband, moved her four children
(D) Jackie's mother Mallie abandoned by her husband moved her four children

62. **(A)** NO CHANGE
(B) Pasadena California, in 1927.
(C) Pasadena, California in 1927.
(D) Pasadena, California, in 1927.

---

61. Ⓐ Ⓑ Ⓒ Ⓓ

62. Ⓐ Ⓑ Ⓒ Ⓓ

Answer #61: Ⓒ

The correct answer is C. "Abandoned by her husband" modifies "Mallie," not "the children" as Answers A and B assert. Answer D omits the necessary commas. **(Sentence structure)**

Answer #62: Ⓓ

The correct answer is D. Commas are necessary to separate the name of a city and a state and to separate a place name from a date. The other answers do not completely correct the errors. **(Punctuation)**

63. **(A)** NO CHANGE
(B) won the junior college championship, and he was named
(C) won the junior college championship and he is named
(D) won the junior college championship, and he named

64. **(A)** NO CHANGE
(B) college's baseball team, and was named the most
(C) colleges' baseball team, and was named the most
(D) colleges' baseball team and was named the most

---

63. (A) (B) (C) (D)

64. (A) (B) (C) (D)

Answer #63: Ⓑ

The correct answer is B. This answer correctly includes a comma to precede the coordinate conjunction "and" that connects the two independent clauses. Answers A and C omit this necessary comma, while Answer C also changes from past to present tense in the second clause. Answer D omits part of the verb "is named," thus changing the meaning of the second clause. Be sure to read all of the answers carefully. **(Sentence structure)**

Answer #64: Ⓐ

The correct answer is A. The singular possessive form of "college" is "college's." Answer B incorrectly inserts a comma between the parts of a compound predicate. Answer C also has this needless comma as well as the plural possessive form of "college," which appears in Answer D as well. **(Sentence structure)**

65. **(A)** NO CHANGE
(B) Too he was on the track team.
(C) He was also on the track team.
(D) And also he was on the track team.

66. **(A)** NO CHANGE
(B) The war began after working for a few years,
(C) The war broke out when he worked for a few years,
(D) After he had worked for a few years, war broke out,

65. (A) (B) (C) (D)

66. (A) (B) (C) (D)

Answer #65: Ⓒ

The correct answer is C. Answer A is repetitive because it includes both "also" and "too." Answer B is awkwardly worded with "Too" at the beginning. Answer D creates a sentence fragment because it begins with a coordinate conjunction. **(Style)**

Answer #66: Ⓓ

The correct answer is D. Answers A and B create dangling modifiers (Did the war work for a few years?). Answer C has a tense sequence error; the events described did not happen at the same time. Answer D correctly uses the past perfect tense for "work" because this action preceded the time when "the war broke out." **(Sentence structure)**

67. The correct order for the sentences in paragraph 3 is:

(A) NO CHANGE
(B) 2, 1, 3, 4, 5
(C) 4, 1, 2, 3, 5
(D) 5, 4, 3, 1, 2

68. **(A)** NO CHANGE
(B) recruits
(C) was recruited
(D) will be recruited

67. (A) (B) (C) (D)

68. (A) (B) (C) (D)

Answer #67: Ⓒ

The correct answer is C. Sentence 4 is needed as transition to indicate this paragraph concerns Robinson's achievements at UCLA. The other answers do not create logical development. **(Organization)**

Answer #68: Ⓒ

The correct answer is C. Answer A shifts from past to present tense. Answer B incorrectly shifts from passive to active voice. Answer D shifts from past to future tense. **(Style)**

69. **(A)** NO CHANGE
(B) 1955 Dodgers, who, finally, after four previous attempts,
(C) 1955 Dodgers. Who, finally, after four previous attempts,
(D) 1955 Dodgers who finally after four previous attempts,

70. **(A)** NO CHANGE
(B) gotten
(C) has gotten
(D) had gotten

69. (A) (B) (C) (D)

70. (A) (B) (C) (D)

Answer #69: Ⓑ

The correct answer is B. Answers A and C each include a sentence fragment, "Who finally after four previous attempts. . . ." Answer D omits a comma after "Dodgers" needed to set off an adjective clause from a proper noun. **(Sentence structure)**

Answer #70: Ⓓ

The correct answer is D. The other answers are incorrect verb forms of the verb "to get." The principal parts of "get" are "get," "got," and "gotten." **(Grammar and usage)**

71. **(A)** NO CHANGE
(B) the Dodgers and Philadelphia were tied
(C) the Dodgers, and Philadelphia was tied
(D) the Dodgers, and Philadelphia were tied

72. **(A)** NO CHANGE
(B) As a result of Jackie Robinson's contributions,
(C) Minus Jackie Robinson's contributions,
(D) So if it were not for the amazing fact of Jackie Robinson's contributions,

---

71. (A) (B) (C) (D)

72. (A) (B) (C) (D)

Answer #71: (B)

The correct answer is B. Answers A and C include subject-verb agreement errors; the plural subject needs a plural verb. Answers C and D incorrectly insert a comma between parts of a compound subject. **(Grammar and usage)**

Answer #72: (A)

The correct answer is A. This choice most concisely expresses the idea. Answers B and D and wordy. Answer C is illogical because "minus" here means "negative." **(Strategy)**

73. **(A)** NO CHANGE
(B) Willie Mays, Hank Aaron or Darryl Strawberry.
(C) Willie Mays Hank Aaron, or Darryl Strawberry.
(D) Willie Mays, Hank Aaron, or Darryl Strawberry.

74. The best description of the author's intent in this passage is to:

(A) explain Jackie Robinson's role in integrating baseball.
(B) compare Jackie Robinson with Bobby Thompson.
(C) describe Jackie Robinson's athletic achievements.
(D) analyze Jackie Robinson's athletic ability.

73. (A) (B) (C) (D)

74. (A) (B) (C) (D)

Answer #73: Ⓓ

The correct answer is D. Items in a series, including the last one, should be separated by commas. The other answers omit needed commas. **(Punctuation)**

Answer #74: Ⓒ

The correct answer is C. Answers A and B are too limited; the passage deals with more than baseball, and Bobby Thompson is mentioned briefly. Answer D is incorrect because the passage does not analyze Robinson's athletic ability. **(Strategy)**

75. The best description of this passage's organization is

(A) spatial
(B) causal
(C) chronological
(D) antithetical

75. (A) (B) (C) (D)

Answer #75: Ⓒ

The correct answer is C. The information as presented offers details in order of the time in which they occurred. Answer A ("spatial") refers to a type of organization that moves from a single point of reference and moves in one direction, such as from north to south or from near to far. Answer B refers to a cause-effect relationship. Answer D ("antithetical") refers to a contrast. **(Organization)**